A Gift for:

_____

From:

_____

A

MESSAGE

of

Comfort

& Hope

EUGENE H. PETERSON

Contents

We Begin with God . . .

*We worship a God
who does things for us
that we cannot do
for ourselves.*

Oh, blessed be God!

He didn't go off and leave us.

He didn't abandon us. . . .

PSALM 124:6

❦

The fundamental mistake is to begin with ourselves and not God. God is the center from which all life develops.

We begin with God.

We dare to believe that God cares who we are, knows who we are.

We dare to believe that God is the reality beyond and beneath and around all things, visible and invisible, and that he provides for us and loves and blesses and saves us.

He heals the heartbroken
and bandages their wounds.

PSALM 147:3

❋

The only serious mistake we can make when illness comes, when anxiety threatens . . . is to conclude that God has gotten bored looking after us and has shifted his attention to a more exciting Christian. Or that God has gotten too busy fulfilling prophecy in the Middle East to take time now to sort out the complicated mess we have gotten ourselves into.

That is the *only* serious mistake we can make.

The moment I called out,

you stepped in; you made my life

large with strength.

PSALM 138:3

❋

"If you'll hold on to me for dear life," says GOD,

    "I'll get you out of any trouble.

I'll give you the best of care

    if you'll only get to know and trust me."

PSALM 91:14

❋

GOD *is good to one and all;*

everything he does is suffused with grace.

PSALM 145:9

❧

God not only speaks to us, he listens to us. His listening to us is an even greater marvel than his speaking to us.

GOD *always does what he says,*
   and is gracious in everything he does.
GOD *gives a hand to those down on their luck,*
   gives a fresh start to those ready to quit.

PSALM 145:13-14

We cannot define God; we cannot package God. But that doesn't mean that we are completely at sea with God, never knowing what to expect, nervously on edge all the time, wondering what he might do.

We know very well what to expect,
      and what we expect is mercy.

Everything GOD *does is right—*

the trademark on all his works is love.

PSALM 145:17

❋

It's wonderful what happens when
Christ displaces worry at the center of your life.

PHILIPPIANS 4:7

We need not muddle through half the day, or half our lives, before God shows up, rubbing his eyes, asking if there is anything he might do for us.

He knows the kind of world we live in and our vulnerability to it. He is there right on time to help.

Like a shepherd, he will care for his flock,

gathering the lambs in his arms,

Hugging them as he carries them,

leading the nursing ewes to good pasture.

Why would you ever complain, O Jacob,

or, whine, Israel, saying,

"GOD has lost track of me.

He doesn't care what happens to me?"

Don't you know anything? Haven't you been listening?

GOD doesn't come and go. God lasts.

He's Creator of all you can see or imagine.

He doesn't get tired out, doesn't pause to catch his breath.

And he knows everything, inside and out.

ISAIAH 40:11, 27

Mostly what God does is love you.

Keep company with him and learn a life of love.

EPHESIANS 5:2

❧

God does not treat us as alien others, lining us up so that he can evaluate our competence or our usefulness or our worth.

He rules, guides, commands, loves us as children whose destinies he carries in his heart.

THIS IS WHO YOU ARE,
YOUR IDENTITY,
LOVED BY GOD.

GOD IS FOR LIFE AND
AGAINST DEATH.

GOD IS FOR LOVE
AND AGAINST HATE.

GOD IS FOR HOPE AND
AGAINST DESPAIR.

God gets down on his knees among us, gets on our level and shares himself with us. He does not reside afar off and send us diplomatic messages; he kneels among us.

God shares himself generously and graciously.

Why are you down in the dumps, dear soul?

Why are you crying the blues?

Fix my eyes on God—

soon I'll be praising again.

He puts a smile on my face.

He's my God.

PSALM 42:5

God is the living center of everything we are and everything we do. He is before, behind, over, beneath everything. If we separate any part of our lives from him, we are left holding an empty bag.

We're in the Wilderness . . .

When I was desperate,
I called out,
and GOD got me out
of a tight spot.

Eugene Peterson ✦ 26

There are times, no matter how thoroughly we're civilized, when we're plunged into the wilderness . . . a circumstantial wilderness. Everything is gong along fine: we've gotten a job, decorated the house, signed up for car payments. And then suddenly there's a radical change in our bodies, or our emotions, or our thinking, or our friends, or our job. We're out of control. We're in the wilderness.

I readily acknowledge that this circumstantial wilderness is a terrible, frightening, and dangerous place; but I also believe it's a place of beauty. There are things to be seen, heard, and experienced in this wilderness that can be seen, heard, and experienced nowhere else.

In the solitude and silence and emptiness of the wilderness, uncluttered and undistracted by what everyone else is saying and doing, we are able to see God's glory where no one else can see it.

The biblical revelation neither explains nor eliminates suffering. It shows, rather, God entering into the life of suffering humanity, accepting and sharing the suffering.

The suffering is there, and where the sufferer is, God is.

It was our pains he carried—
our disfigurements, all the things wrong with us.
We thought he brought it on himself,
that God was punishing him for his own failures.
But it was our sins that did that to him,
that ripped and tore and crushed him—our sins!
He took the punishment, and that made us whole.
Through his bruises we get healed.

ISAIAH 53:4-5

No test or temptation that comes your way
is beyond the course of what others have had to face.
All you need to remember is that
God will never let you down; he'll never let you be
pushed past your limit; he'll always be there
to help you come through it.

1 CORINTHIANS 10:13

Unpleasant things happen to us. We lose what we think we cannot live without. Pain comes to those we love, and we conclude that there is no justice. Why does God permit this?

Anxiety seeps into our hearts.

But nothing counter to God's justice has any eternity to it.

God knows when to say, enough.

We are secure. God is running the show.

My help and glory are in God
—granite-strength and safe-harbor-God
So trust him absolutely, people;
Lay your lives on the line for him.
God is a safe place to be.

PSALM 62:7–8

The Psalms were prayed by people who understood that God had everything to do with them.
God, not their feelings, was the center.

Let my cry come right into your presence, GOD;

provide me with the insight that comes only from your Word.

Give my request your personal attention,

rescue me on the terms of your promise.

Let praise cascade off my lips;

after all, you've taught me the truth about life!

And let your promises ring from my tongue;

every order you've given is right.

Put your hand out and steady me

since I've chosen to live by your counsel.

PSALM 119:169-173

For the person who suffers, has suffered or will suffer, Psalm 130 is essential equipment, for it convinces us that the big difference is not in what people suffer but in the way they suffer. The psalm does not exhort us to put up with suffering; it does not explain it or explain it away. It is, rather, a powerful demonstration that our place in the depths is not out of bounds from God.

We see that whatever or whoever got us in trouble, cannot separate us from God.

Help, GOD—the bottom has fallen out of my life!

Master, hear my cry for help!

Listen hard! Open your ears!

Listen to my cries for mercy. . . .

I pray to GOD—my life a prayer—

and wait for what he'll say and do. . . .

My life's on the line before God, my Lord,

waiting and watching till morning,

waiting and watching till morning.

PSALM 130:1–6

In suffering we . . . are near to where Christ was on the cross.

Our God, who is characterized by steadfast love and plenteous redemption, is not indifferent to our suffering.

God seeks the hurt, maimed, wandering, and lost.

We stand in confident awe before God.

Eugene Peterson ❦ *38*

No one's ever seen or heard anything like this,

never so much as imagined anything quite like it—

what God has arranged for those who love him.

1 CORINTHIANS 2:9

❦

TO BELIEVE IN A MIRACLE IS ONLY
A WAY OF SAYING THAT GOD IS FREE—
FREE TO DO A NEW THING.

Human beings are in trouble most of the time. Those who don't know they are in trouble are in the most trouble.

Prayer is the language of the people who are in trouble and know it, and who believe or hope that God can get them out.

We Pray and
God Listens . . .

Nowhere in the Bible is there any attempt to answer the question, "Why does a good God permit evil?" Evil is a fact.

The Bible does not provide an explanation of evil—rather, it defines a context: all evil takes place in an historical arena bounded by Christ and prayer.

I found myself in trouble
and went looking for my Lord:

My life was an open wound
that wouldn't heal.

PSALM 77:2

IT IS BETTER TO PRAY BADLY
THAN NOT TO PRAY AT ALL.

GOD, *listen! Listen to my prayer,*
listen to the pain in my cries.

PSALM 102:1

Will the Lord walk off and leave us for good?
Will he never smile again?
Is his love worn threadbare?
Has his salvation promise burned out?
Has God forgotten his manners?
Has he angrily stalked off and left us?
"Just my luck," I said. "The High God goes out of
　　business just the moment I need him."
Once again I'll go over what GOD has done,
lay out on the table the ancient wonders;
I'll ponder all the things you've accomplished,
and give a long, loving look at your acts.
O God! Your way is holy!
No god is great like God!

Any place is the right place to begin to pray. But we must not be afraid of ending up some place quite different from where we start. The psalmist began by feeling sorry for himself and asking questions that seethed with insolence. He ended up singing an old song proclaiming might and grace.

THERE ISN'T A SINGLE
AREA OF OUR LIVES IN WHICH
WE'RE SELF-SUFFICIENT.
WE NEED GOD.

❋

"I pray only
when I am in trouble;
but I am in trouble all the time
so I pray all the time."
—ISAAC BASHEVIS SINGER

God listens.

Everything we say, every groan, every murmur, every stammering attempt at prayer: all this is listened to.

Real help comes from GOD.
Your blessing clothes your people!

PSALM 3:8

Then David took his shepherd's staff,

selected five smooth stones from the brook,

and put them in the pocket of his shepherd's pack,

and with his sling in his hand

approached Goliath.

1 SAMUEL 17:40

❉

T he text doesn't say that David knelt, . . . but he must have knelt to select the stones. I see him kneeling.

Until David walked into the Valley of Elah and knelt at that brook, the only options seemed to be a bullying Might or a fearful Right. Take your choice: brutal Goliath or anxious Saul.

David kneeling, unhurried and calm, opened up another option: God. God's ways, God's salvation.

David entered the Valley of Elah with a God-dominated, not a Goliath dominated, imagination.

Tending his father's sheep, David . . . had experienced God's strength in protecting the sheep in his fights with lions and bears. He had practiced the presence of God so thoroughly that God's word, which he couldn't literally hear, was far more real to him than the lion's roar, which he could hear.

In prayer we intend to leave the world of anxieties and enter a world of wonder.

We decide to leave an ego-centered world and enter a God-centered world.

We will to leave a world of problems and enter a world of mystery.

But it is not easy. We are used to anxieties, egos, and problems; we are not used to wonder, God, and mystery.

Let petitions and praises shape your
worries into prayers,
letting God know your concerns.

PHILIPPIANS 4:6

HOPE IS A RESPONSE TO
THE FUTURE THAT HAS ITS FOUNDATION
IN THE PROMISES OF GOD.

Pile your troubles on GOD*'s shoulders
—he'll carry your load, he'll help you out.*

PSALM 55:22

IT IS EASY TO BE HONEST
BEFORE GOD WITH OUR HALLELUJAHS;
IT IS SOMEWHAT MORE DIFFICULT
TO BE HONEST IN OUR HURTS;
IT IS NEARLY IMPOSSIBLE TO BE
HONEST BEFORE GOD IN
THE DARK EMOTIONS OF OUR HATE.
IN PRAYER, ALL IS
NOT SWEETNESS AND LIGHT.

I bless GOD *every chance I get;*

my lungs expand with his praise.

PSALM 34:1

※

All prayer, pursued far enough, becomes praise. No matter how much we suffer, no matter our doubts, no matter how angry we get, no matter how many times we have asked in desperation or doubt, "How long?", prayer develops finally into praise. Everything finds its way to the doorstep of praise.

Praise is the consummating prayer.

You, G<small>OD</small>, are sovereign still,

always and ever sovereign.

PSALM 102:12

❦

Hoping is not dreaming. It is not spinning an illusion or fantasy to protect us from our boredom or our pain. It means a confident, alert expectation that God will do what he said he will do.

It is a willingness to let God do it his way and in his time.

Hoping does not mean doing nothing. It is not fatalistic resignation. It means going about our assigned tasks, confident that God will provide the meaning and the conclusions. It is the opposite of desperate and panicky manipulations, of scurrying and worrying.

Silence is praise to you,

    Zion-dwelling God,

And also obedience.

    You hear the prayer in it all.

PSALM 65:1–2

My soul waits.
Another will is greater,
wiser and more intelligent than my own.
So I wait. Waiting means there is
another whom I trust and
from whom I receive.

*Put your hope in GOD
and know real blessing!*

PSALM 146:5

❦

God Is Beside Us...

God is a safe place to hide,
ready to help when we need him.

PSALM 46:1

People of faith have the same needs for protection and security as anyone else. We are no better than others in that regard. What is different is that we find that we don't have to build our own: "God is a safe place to hide, ready to help when we need him."

God is at our side.

God's loyal love couldn't have run out,

his merciful love couldn't have dried up.

They're created new every morning.

How great your faithfulness!

I'm sticking with God (I say it over and over).

He's all I've got left.

LAMENTATIONS 3:22-24

✳

The God who created heaven
and earth helps us personally.
The One who pulled a universe
into order and beauty, this same
God is involved in the local troubles
of a quite ordinary person.

Your love, GOD, fills the earth!
Train me to live by your counsel.

PSALM 119:64

❋

Thank GOD! He deserves your thanks.
His love never quits.

PSALM 136:1

❋

The spacious, free life is from GOD,
it's also protected and safe.
GOD-strengthened, we're delivered from evil—
when we run to him, he saves us.

PSALM 37:39-40

When we sin and mess up our lives, we find that God doesn't go off and leave us—he enters into our trouble and saves us.

Thank the Lord
of all lords.
His love never quits.

PSALM 136:3

We are told repeatedly in Scripture to "trust God." We are asked to assume confidently that He will work in us and in the world powerfully and victoriously. But who can engage in such trust?

God calls us; we answer.

God forgives us; we accept His forgiveness.

God acts toward us in a way that draws forth our trust; and we trust Him.

Christians learn to trust God not because they have been convinced by arguments that they should trust Him but because they have been treated by God in a loving, accepting, trusting way before they were lovable, acceptable, or trustworthy.

First we were loved,

now we love.

He loved us first.

1 JOHN 4:19

THE LIVING GOD PERSONALLY ADDRESSES
AND MERCIFULLY FORGIVES US.
HE SETS THINGS RIGHT AT THE CENTER.
THAT IS WHAT WE NEED,
WHAT WE WANT.

Eugene Peterson ✷ 72

GOD is sheer mercy and grace;

not easily angered, he's rich in love.

He doesn't endlessly nag and scold,

nor hold grudges forever.

He doesn't treat us as our sins deserve,

nor pay us back in full for our wrongs.

As high as heaven is over the earth,

so strong is his love to those who fear him.

And as far as sunrise is from sunset,

he has separated us from our sins.

As parents feel for their children,

GOD feels for those who fear him.

PSALM 103:8-13

God assured us,

"I'll never let you down,

never walk off and leave you."

HEBREWS 13:5

❊

The almond tree is one of the earliest trees to bloom in Palestine. Before it puts forth leaves, it puts forth blossoms, white and snowy. While the land is still chill from winter, the warm blossoms, untended and unforced, surprise us with a promise of spring. Every spring it happens again.

The blossom is a delight in itself, beautiful to look at, fragrant to smell. But it is more. It is anticipation. It is promise. Like words. God's words are not mere words. They are promises that lead to fulfillment. God performs what he announces. God does what he says.

I have it all planned out—
plans to take care of you,
not abandon you,
plans to give you the future
you hope for.

JEREMIAH 29:11

Hope acts on the conviction that God will complete the work he has begun even when the appearances, especially when the appearances, oppose it.

It is, of course, far easier to languish in despair than to live in hope, for when we live in despair we don't have to do anything or risk anything. If we live in hope, we go against the stream.

BECAUSE GOD FREELY KEEPS
HIS PROMISES,
WE ARE FREE TO TRUST.

GOD WIPES
AWAY OUR TEARS...

Joy comes because God knows how to wipe away tears, and, in his resurrection work, create the smile of new life.

GOD is good to one and all;
everything he does
is suffused with grace.

PSALM 145:9

❋

GOD'S WAYS AND GOD'S PRESENCE
ARE WHERE WE EXPERIENCE THE
HAPPINESS THAT LASTS.

Every detail in our
lives of love for God is worked
into something good.

ROMANS 8:28

Christian joy is not an escape from sorrow. Pain and hardship still come, but they are unable to drive out the happiness of the redeemed.

Joy is what God gives, not what we work up.

Laughter is the delight that things are working together for good to those who love God.

*Those who went off with
heavy hearts will come home laughing,
with armloads of blessing*

PSALM 126:6

Joy is nurtured by anticipation. If the joy-producing acts of God are characteristic of our past as God's people, they will also be characteristic of our future as his people. There is no reason to suppose that God will arbitrarily change his way of working with us. What we have known of him, we will know of him.

Just as joy builds on the past, it borrows from the future.

You who fear GOD,

trust in GOD!—

trust your Helper!

Thank you! Everything in me says "Thank you!"

Angels listen as I sing my thanks.

I kneel in worship facing your holy temple

and say it again: "Thank you!"

Thank you for your love,

thank you for your faithfulness;

most holy is your name,

most holy is your Word.

PSALM 138:1-2

❋

GOD's strong name is our help,

the same GOD who made heaven and earth.

PSALM 124:8

Faith develops out of the most difficult aspects of our existence, not the easiest.

We speak our words of praise in a world that is hellish; we sing our songs of victory in a world where things get messy; we live our joy among people who neither understand nor encourage us. But the content of our lives is God, not humanity.

God will do things in you that neither you nor your friends would have supposed possible. He is not limited by anything you think you know about him; he is not boxed into the cramped dimensions of your ignorance or your despair.

Like an open book,
you watched me grow
from conception to birth;
all the stages of my life were
spread out before you.

PSALM 139:16

❋

Do you think anyone is going
to be able to drive a wedge between us
and Christ's love for us? There is no way!
Not trouble, not hard times, not hatred, not hunger,
not homelessness, not bullying threats,
not backstabbing, not even
the worst sins listed in Scripture.
Absolutely nothing can
get between us and God's love.

ROMANS 8:35, 39

I don't know one thing about the future.

I don't know what the next hour will hold. There may be sickness, accident, personal or world catastrophe. Before this day is over I may have to deal with death, pain, loss, rejection. I don't know what the future holds for me, for those I love, for my nation, for this world.

Still, despite my ignorance and surrounded by tinny optimists and cowardly pessimists, I say that God will accomplish his will, and I cheerfully persist in living in the hope that nothing will separate me from Christ's love.

You call out to God

for help and he helps.

1 PETER 1:17